ARTIST TRANSCRIPTIONS PIANO

BLUES PIANO LEGENDS

ISBN 978-1-4803-0455-0

HAL•LEONARD®
CORPORATION

7777 W. BLUEMOUND RD. P.O. BOX 13819 MILWAUKEE, WI 53213

Visit Hal Leonard Online at
www.halleonard.com

DISCOGRAPHY

SONG	PIANIST	ALBUM
Big Chief	Professor Longhair	*Louisiana Piano Rhythms*
Bloody Murder	Otis Spann	Muddy Waters – *Muddy*
(The Original) Boogie Woogie	Pinetop Perkins	*Pinetop is Just Top*
Boogie Woogie Stomp	Albert Ammons	*The First Day*
Chicago Breakdown	Big Maceo	*The Very Best of Boogie Woogie*
Confessin' the Blues	Jay McShann	*Last of the Blue Devils*
Driftin' Blues	Charles Brown	*Pioneers of Rhythm & Blues Vol. 2*
Every Day I Have the Blues	Memphis Slim	*The Sonnet Blues Story*
44 Blues	Roosevelt Sykes	*Piano Boogie Woogie Vol. 1*
Got My Mo Jo Working	Jay McShann	*Best of the Straight-Up Blues*
Honky Tonk Train	Meade "Lux" Lewis	*Honky Tonk Train Blues*
I Just Want to Make Love to You	Otis Spann	Muddy Waters – *Muddy*
Mess Around	Ray Charles	*Mess Around*
Swanee River Boogie	Albert Ammons	*Boogie Woogie Showcase Vol. 4*
Two Fisted Mama	Katie Webster	*Deluxe Edition*
Worried Life Blues	Big Maceo	*The Complete Sides*

Big Chief

By Earl King

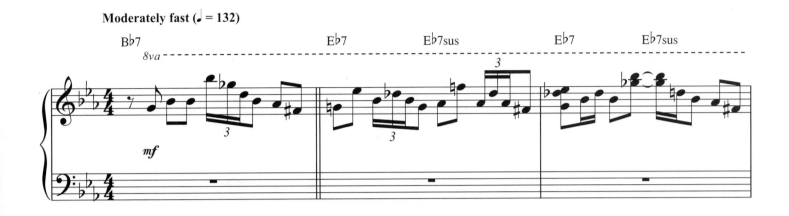

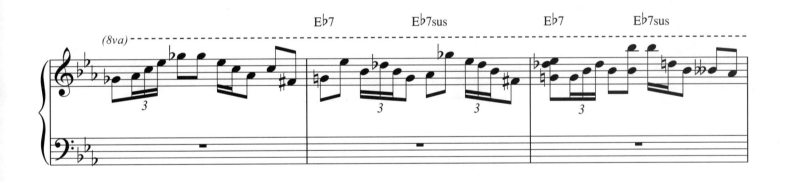

Me ___ got a fire me can't put out.

Heap ___ fire wa-ter gon-na make me shout. ___

Me ___ go-ing down and get my squaw.

Me ___ might buy great big horse.

Me ___ gon-na do ev-'ry-thing me could.

Me ___ big chief, I'm feel-ing good.

Bloody Murder

By Otis Spann

Moderately slow (♩ = 60)

Call it blood-y mur-der. ___ Blood ___ stained all o - ver the wall. ___

Well now, you know it,

call it blood-y mur-der. ___ There were blood-stains ___ all o-ver the

wall. _

Sheets and pil-lows torn to piec-es, and my phone was hang-ing out in the hall. _

I won-der what could've hap-pened to my ba-by. Don't know hard-ly where'd _ my ba - by go. ____

Won-der what hap-pened to my ba - by. Won-der where's _____ my ba-by gone. ____

It was ear - ly one mor - ning, Lord, ___ my ba - by, I told ___ you I was home. ___

Lord, have mer - cy, _____

Lord, have mer-cy on me. _____

Please, Lord, _____ have mer - cy,

I said, Lord, __ have mer - cy on me.

If an - y - bod y's seen my ba - by,

please send that wom - an home to me. __

(The Original)
Boogie Woogie

Music by Clarence "Pine Top" Smith

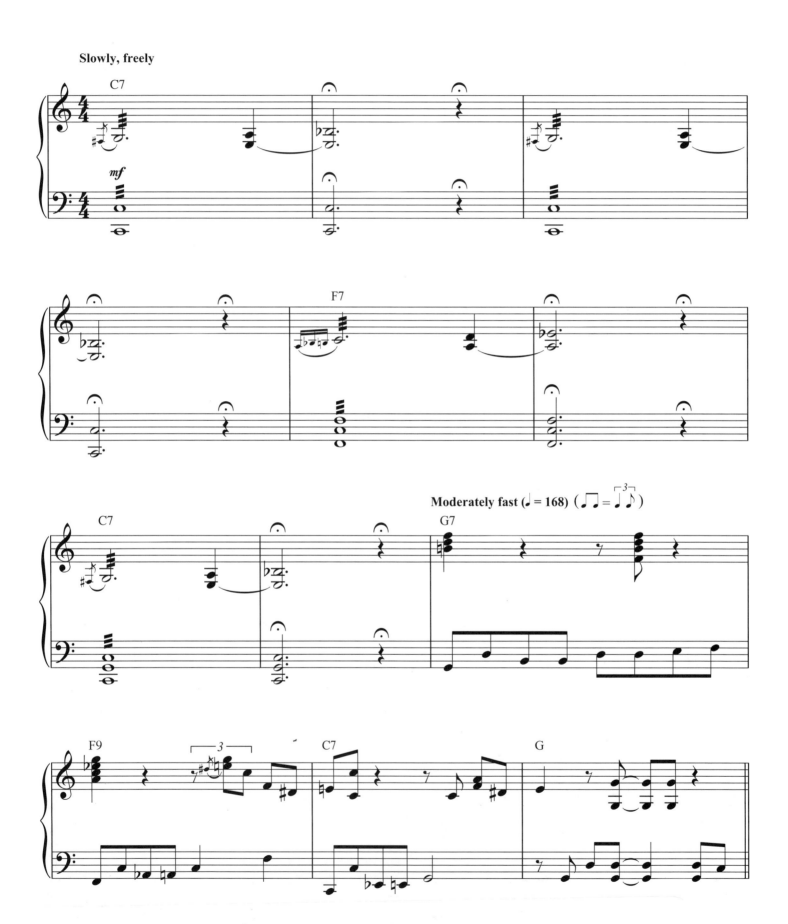

24

Now I don't want y'all to forget, you know, that Mister Pinetop's boogie woogie;   *do it just like I tell you.*

Boogie Woogie Stomp

Words and Music by Albert Ammons

Chicago Breakdown

By Maceo Meriweather

48

Confessin' the Blues

Words and Music by Walter Brown and Jay McShann

I'd rath - er love you, ba - by,

more than an - y - one else in town. ___

Be - cause you're so nice and lov - ing, and you

have such pleas - ing ways, ___ take me to your home; ___ be there,

be rest of my days. ___ That's the truth, ma - ma.

Well, you know ___ I ___ was - n't ly - ing;

'cause if I don't love you, ba - by, ___

well I swear ___ I hope to die.

Well, ba - by, ___ don't you want a man _ like

me? Yeah, _ ba - by, _____

don't you want a man _ like _ me. ___ Just think

a-bout your fu - ture; for - get a-bout, _ your "used to be." ___

Now when my

ba - by,   can I have you for my - self? ___

You were ___ meant ___

___ for me, ma - ma's; ___   I don't want ___ no - bod - y else. ___

Oh yeah. ___

Got My Mo Jo Working

Words and Music by Preston Foster

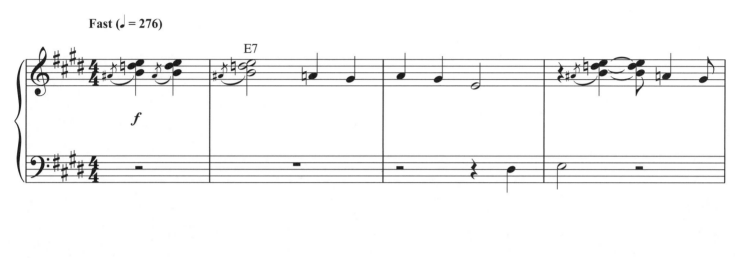

Bass arranged for piano L.H.

work - ing, but it   just ___ don't   work on ___ you.

I ___ wan - na love you so bad, ___

___ 'til I   don't ___ know   what   to   do. ___

I'm ___ go - ing

down in Loui - si - an - a to   get me a

mo - jo, hey.

I'm __ go - ing down in Loui - si -

a - na to   get me a mo - jo, hey.

I'm _____ gon - na have all you wom - en wretched __ un - der my com - mand. __

Got _____ my

(Got ___ my mo - jo
mo - jo work - ing.

work - ing.)
Got my mo - jo work - ing, but it

just ___ don't work on you.

Harmonica solo

(Solo ends)

Got ___ my mo - jo ___ work - ing. ___ (Got ___ my

mo - jo work - ing.) Got ___ my mo - jo ___ work - ing. ___

(Got ___ my mo - jo work - ing.) (Bbbbb, _____

(Got ___ my mo - jo

___ it's work - ing!

work-ing.)
Got ___ my mo - jo ___ work-ing. ___ (Got ___ my

mo - jo work-ing.) mo - jo
Got ___ my

Slowly, freely

work-ing, but it just don't work on you. ___

Moderately slow (♩. = 63)

Driftin' Blues

Words and Music by Charles Brown, Johnny Moore and Eddie Williams

would on - ly take me back a - gain. _____

If my ba - by _____

would on - ly take me back a - gain. _____

No, I'm not good for noth-in'. _____

Well, I have - n't got no friends. _____

Guitar solo ad lib.

I give you all ___ my mon-ey.

Tell me, what more can I do? ___

Bye-bye, ba - by. ____ Ba-by, bye - bye, ____ bye - bye. ____

Bye - bye, ba - by, ____

Every Day I Have the Blues

Words and Music by Peter Chatman

day and ev -'ry night, ev -'ry-day I ___ have the blues.

So when you see ___

___ me wor-ry- ing, peo - ple, you know it's you that I hate to lose. ___

No - bod - y loves ___

luck and trou - ble, peo - ple, do you know, do you know I've had my

share? Now I'm gon - na

pack my suit - case, __ gon - na move on down the line. __

I'm __ gon -

na pack my suit - case. Yes, I'm mov - ing on ____ down ___ the line. ___

Know that no -

- bod - y wor - ry - ing; don't ___ see ____ no - bod - y cry -

ing.

44 Blues

Words and Music by Roosevelt Sykes

Moderately fast, freely (♩ = 152)

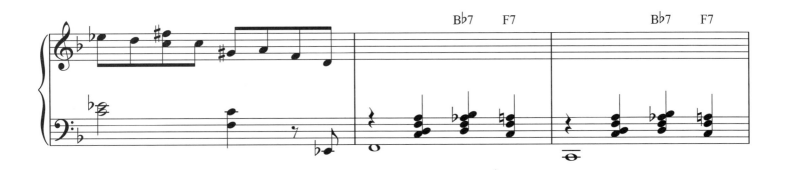

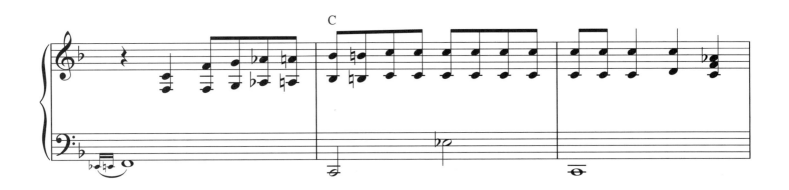

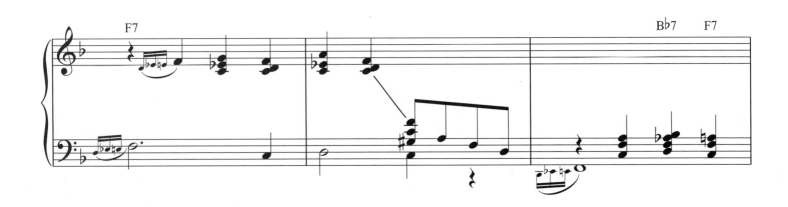

Lord, I walked all ___ night long ___ with

my ___ for - ty four ___ in my hands.

Now I ___

___ walked all night long with my for - ty four ___

93

in my hand.

I was look - ing for my wom - an,

found _____ her with an - oth - er man.

Lord, I wore my for-ty four so long, _____

Lord, it made my shoul-der sore. _____

Lord, I wore my _____

_____ for-ty four so long, _____ Lord, it made my _____

shoul - der sore.

After I do what I want to,

ain't gon - na wear my for - ty four

no more.

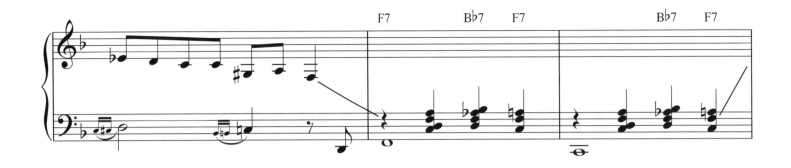

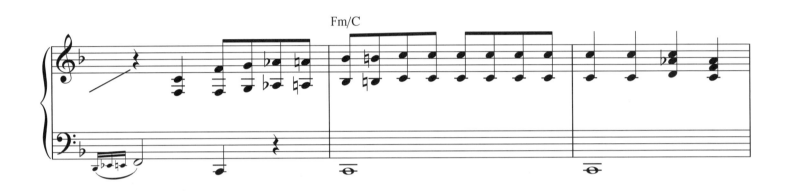

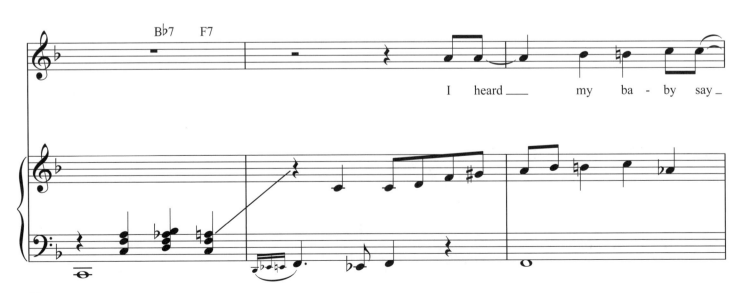

I heard ___ my ba - by say ___

she heard that for-ty four whis-tle blow. _

I heard my ba-by say _____ she

heard that for-ty four whis-tle blow. _

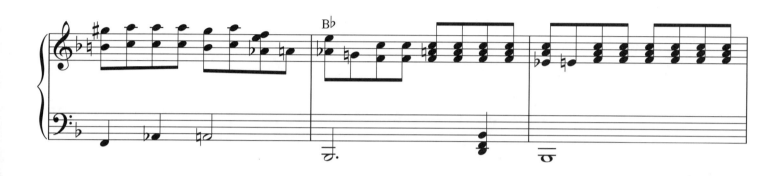
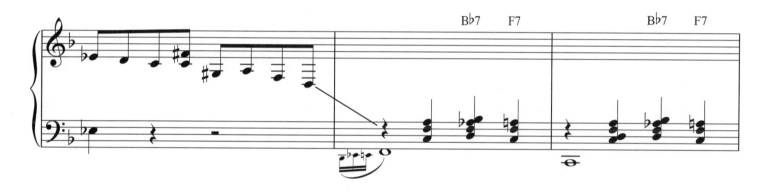
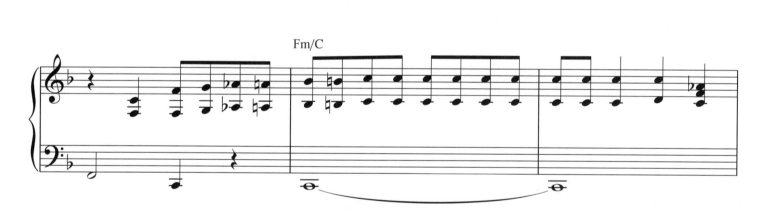

Now I've got a lit - tle cab -

in, Lord, it's num - ber for - ty four. ___

Lord, I've got a lit - tle cab - in,

I Just Want to Make Love to You

Written by Willie Dixon

love — to you,　love to you,　love to you.

Harmonica solo

I tell by the way you
switch and walk, ___ I can see by the way you

Bass arranged for piano L.H.

I don't want, __ be - cause I'm sad and blue; __

I just want to make love to you, love to you,

(begin fadeout)

love to you, love to you, love to you,

love to you, love to you.

(fadeout complete)

Mess Around

Words and Music by Ahmet Ertegun

Ah, ___ you can

talk a-bout the pit bar - be-cue. The band was jump-in',

the peo-ple too. Ah, mess a - round,

they're do - ing the mess a - round.

They're do - ing the mess a - round.

mess a - round.   They're do - ing the

mess a - round.   Ev - 'ry - bod - y do - ing the mess a -

round.   Now, __ ah,

when I say __ stop, don't you __ move a peg, __ but when

I say go, just, __ ah, shake __ your leg and do the

mess a - round.

I de - clare, ____ do - ing the

mess a - round. __

Yeah, __ do the

mess a - round.

Ev - 'ry - bod - y's do - ing the mess a -

(Saxophone solo)

mess a - round.   They're do - ing the   mess a - round.

Ev - 'ry - bod - y's   do - ing the   mess a - round.

Now ___ you   see   that ___   girl ___ with   that

dia - mond   ring?   She ___ knows   how   to

Swanee River Boogie

Music by Hattie Young

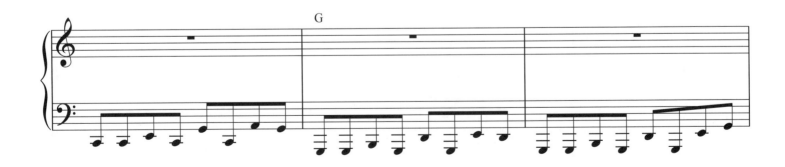

(Piano R.H. as recorded)

Two Fisted Mama

Words and Music by Bruce Iglauer and Kathryn Thorne

'cause I've messed __ up the best. ____

'Cause I'm a two-fist-ed ma-ma; I ain't like all the rest,... __

____ *Spoken:* *...and you'd better believe that.*

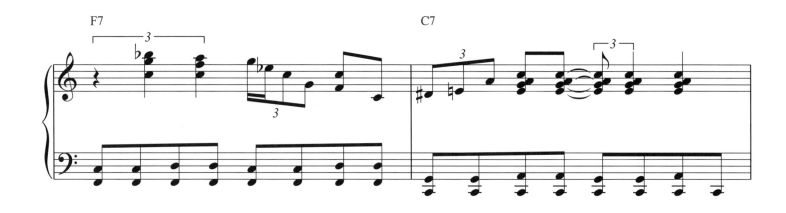

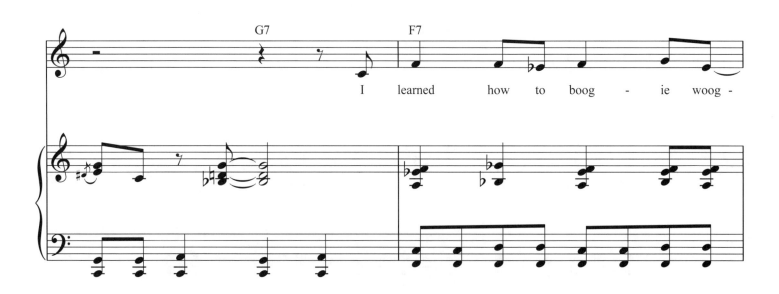

I learned how to boog - ie woog -

took ma all a-round the world. ___ I taught this old pi-a-

- no how to shake, rat-tle and roll. ___ I took the

blues from Hous-ton, Tex - as; I gave the world my soul; __

___ 'cause I'm a two-fist-ed ma-ma; you just grab a hold. __

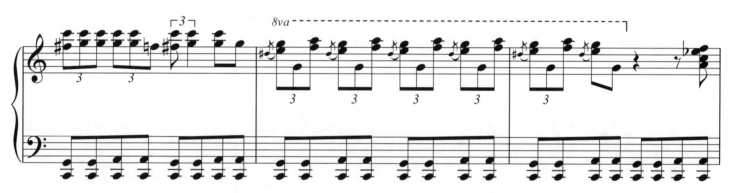

137

Worried Life Blues
Words and Music by Maceo Merriweather

ba - by, ___ I ain't gon - na wor - ry my life no ___

more. _____ So man - y nights ___

since ___ you've been gone, _____ I've ___ been wor -

ried and griev - ing ___ my ___ life a - lone; ___ but some - day,

139

ba - by, ___

I ain't gon-na wor - ry my life an-y

more. ___

So that's _ my sto - ry. This is all I've _

got to say _____ to you: good - bye, _ ba-by, _____ and I don't _ care what you

do. _____ But some - day, ba - by, _____

I ain't gon-na wor - ry my life an-y more. _____

Honky Tonk Train

(Honky Tonk Train Blues)

By Meade (Lux) Lewis

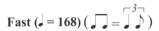

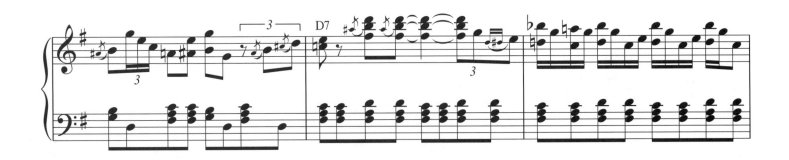